CREDIT REPAIR SECRETS

The Secret Steps To Repair Your Credit Score
And Increase Your Score Thanks To The
609 Letters Included

ANDREW BENNET

Introduction

You're here because you want to know how credit repair works. We're not going to beat around the bush with you. Credit repair isn't easy work and it won't be a quick process either. You've done the preliminary legwork in trying to get your finances back in order by setting financial targets, creating a schedule, seeking ways to save money, and requesting a copy of your credit report. Now that you have a copy of your credit report from one of the three credit reporting agencies, it's time to roll up your sleeves and fix the misleading details on your credit report.

What Is Credit Repair and How Does It Work?

Credit repair is the method of repairing credit status that has degraded due to a number of factors. It could be as simple as disputing the details to improve your credit score. Another type of credit repair is to address financial issues such as budgeting and begin to address concerns.

Significant Points to consider

• Credit repair is the method of raising or repairing one's credit score.

• Paying a company to contact the credit bureau and point out something in your report that is misleading or wrong, and demanding that it be deleted, is another choice for credit repair.

How Credit Repair Works

While businesses claim to be able to clean up bad credit reports, doing so takes time and effort. The details cannot be removed by a third party. Specifics that are wrong or misrepresented may be challenged. If their credit reports contain inaccurate or incomplete information, they can file a dispute. Fixing and repairing credit may have a greater impact on credit usage and action than correcting such advice or catching fraudulent trades on one's credit. This person's payment background may have an effect on their credit score. Taking steps to ensure that payments are made on time or to improve the payment program for unpaid credit can have a negative effect on their credit score. The total amount of credit you have could be a factor. For example, if someone is knowingly using large amounts of credit available to them, even if they are making minimum payments on time, the size of their debt may have a negative impact on their credit score. The issue is that their liquidity can be influenced by their debt. They could see results if they took action to reduce their debt.

Creditors Can Help

If you have a long-standing account with a creditor, you can also contact them directly to clarify the mistake on your credit report. Request that they write you a letter containing the email and the correction. In addition, request that they notify each credit reporting agency that has received this incorrect entry in order to correct it.

Create a copy of the letter and attach it to the letter of dispute you send after the creditor receives a copy. Submit it to the credit reporting service and ask them to update their records. The credit reporting agency will send you a new credit report after it is done.

Chapter 1. Is Credit Repair Bad and Ethical?

Beware, not all credit repair companies are ethical. Do not fall for scams that promise they can take a bad credit record and turn it around overnight. Or that guarantee they can "force" the credit bureaus to remove all negative (but accurate) information from your credit file immediately. It takes time and your cooperation to improve your credit. Trust me when I tell you that a credit repair company cannot push around the large credit bureaus. Never mind order them to do things like immediately remove foreclosures or missed payments from the records of their client's. Inaccurate information can be easily fixed. However, removing accurate negative information takes a plan and is rarely done overnight. That usually requires filing official disputes, and careful negotiations with your creditors.

Some credit repair companies not only misrepresent what they can do for you, but also practice illegal or fraudulent ways of trying to improve your credit. Often, they will reorganize as a non-profit to get around state and federal laws that govern the industry. If you are desperate enough, you may be tempted to risk some of these illegal actions, but we would not recommend it. People have lost hundreds, and in some cases thousands of dollars to credit repair scams.

The Warning Signs When Choosing a Credit Repair Company

-They recommend that you do not contact credit bureaus directly.

-They do not disclose your legal rights or what you can do yourself.

-They want you to pay upfront based on their verbal promises before they do any work. They can only charge you after they have completed the services they contracted for.

-They suggest unethical or illegal actions such as making false statements on a loan application, misrepresenting your social security number, or obtaining an EIN number under false pretensions. The use of these tactics could constitute general fraud, civil fraud, mail fraud, wire fraud, and get you into a lot of trouble.

The Disputing Process

The first thing you need to know is that all three credit reporting agencies have to contest the inaccurate information independently. The disputed appearance may be on all three credit reports or may not. Keep in mind that customers may not belong to all credit reporting agencies. This is why you will see that on one list some of the investors are not on the others.

Even though all three credit reporting agencies have the same information, this does not mean that if an item comes out of one credit report it will come out of the others. No promise is provided what the outcome will be. That is why you have to refute any inaccurate information about each particular article.

They can use their appeal forms when disputing with credit reporting agencies, write your own message, or challenge the item online on their Website. If you decide to dispute by letter-writing, simply state the facts in a simple, concise or two sentences. If you choose to write a personalized message, you can also use the same answers as appropriate. Sample answers would be:

- This is not my account.

- This was not late as indicated.

- This was not charged off.

- This was paid off in full as agreed.

- This was not a collection account.

- This is not my bankruptcy as indicated.

- This is not my tax lien as indicated.

- This is not my judgment as indicated.

If you have found more than four entries on your credit  report that you need to dispute, do not dispute everything in one letter. Whether you are writing a letter, filling out their form or answering via the Internet, break your disputes. You send or go back every 30 days to the website of the credit reporting agency and challenge up to four more things. On submitting each address, expect to receive a revised credit report about

45 days after you send your letter or disagreement online. If your new credit report has not been issued before it is time to appeal the second time, go ahead and mail your second letter or challenge online instead.

Once all the grievance letters have been mailed or posted to their website and all the revised credit reports have been received, check whether products have been omitted or incomplete. If you need to do the procedure again for the remaining items, space 120 days from your most recent update for another disputes.

What you should not do:

- Alter your identity or try to change it.

- The story is fictional.

- Check any information which is 100% correct.

What you should do:

- Read your emails, should you decide to send them to us? If a letter looks legitimate, credit reporting agencies will believe it has been written by a credit repair service, and they will not investigate the dispute.

- Use your original letterhead (if you do have one).

- Use the appeal form included with the credit report by the credit reporting agency, if you want.

- Provide some evidence suggesting the wrong entry is erroneous.

- Include the identification number for all communications listed on the credit report.

Spotting Possible Identity Theft

Checking your credit report could also spot potential identity theft. That is why you should inquire at least once a year or every six months for a copy of your credit report.

Things to look for would be:

- Names of accounts and figures that you do not know.

- You do not remember filling out loan applications.

- Addresses you did not live in.

- Poor bosses or tenants' enquiries you do not know.

Credit Rescoring

Rapid rescoring is an expedited way of fixing anomalies in the credit file of a customer. A fast rescore dispute process works through borrowers and mortgage brokers, a number of approved registry credit reporting companies, and credit reporting agencies.

If you are a creditor applying for a rescore on your credit report, you would need to provide detailed documents that would be sent to the collateral agencies that are working on your case. Cash registry is the system used by cash grantors. The data archive gathers the records from the three main credit reporting agencies and has to check the consumer's initial information for a rescore. Once the verification is entered into the program of the repository a new score will be produced.

The downside of a fast rescore is that you save money

without having to contend individually with a credit reporting agency that may take longer than 30 days to complete an audit. If the sale of a house or lease depends on your credit score, and you are in a time crunch, the best solution is to easily rescore.

First Step in Actually Repairing Your Credit

Write letters to the agencies with the correct but bad items you have encountered and your reasoning for which you think they should be taken off your credit report. The most important thing when writing these letters and when making any type of contact with the people at the credit report agencies is to keep communication very polite and professional. The more pleasant and prepared you are, the more you increase the chances of them helping you repair your credit. Sign and date your letters and try to write them by hand.

Contact with the Creditor

At this point, you have to write another letter, this time to the creditor. You can continue claiming that the negative information is wrong but be warned that they will not believe you if you do not provide solid proof to back up your claim. If you do not think you can muster up that proof in order to make a good case for re-establishing your good credit.

Chapter 2. Secrets Steps of Credit Repair

Step 1: Know your credit score

First things first, see what your credit score is and check your credit report. Most people will tell you that you can check your credit report for free once a year by visiting www.AnnualCreditReport.com. Also, if you are trying to fix your credit score, you will need to check your report at least once a month, not once a year. Other people might also direct you to sources that charge you for checking your credit score or that hurt your credit score every time you check it. Do not do that.

Following is a list of FREE resources where you can check your credit score without having to worry about it costing a thing or hurting your credit:

- www.creditkarma.com – use this site when fixing your credit score. The site provides free credit reports and scores from Equifax and Transunion that are updated every week.

- www.creditsesame.com - Same as credit karma but updates every month instead of week. It gives you a free credit score, but not a free credit report.
- www.quizzle.com - offers a free credit report and score every 3 months.
- www.credit.com - You get two free credit reports and your score is updated once a month.
- www.wallethub.com - gives daily updates to its free credit scores and reports. There are some more websites out there, but these are the most popular.

Once you have signed up with one of these sites and checked your credit score, it is time to analyze your credit report for errors.

Step 2: Thoroughly scan your credit report

Everyone has three credit reports: one from Experian, one from Equifax, and one from Transunion. These are the three big credit bureaus.

Once you get your free report, thoroughly go over it. Is everything correct? Remember, it is actually quite common for mistakes to be on your credit report. It is very important for you to highlight any errors these should be removed from your report, which will increase your credit score

When going through record put these in mind. Are all of my accounts listed? Is my personal information correct? Are all missed and/or late payments correctly listed? Is there anything I do not recognize? Are there still accounts listed that are decades-old? Go over every single thing.

Step 3: Fixing errors on your credit report

First, go over all missed/late payments. Check if you recognize it. If not, dispute it. Have you paid it already? Dispute it. Is the payment more than 7 years old? Dispute it. Other people are inclined to tell you that you need to pay your missed payments and collections so you can just be done with it.

Then check the inquires done on your credit. Dispute any incorrect or unauthorized inquires. Same goes for collections and public records. This is one of the secrets of fixing bad credit. Before disputing, make sure that you are not disputing something that is positively influencing your credit score. Only dispute personal information, credit inquiries, charge offs, collections, bankruptcies, foreclosures, repossessions, tax liens, judgments and others.

But how exactly do you dispute a charge? For every error, you need to dispute it by all three credit bureaus. I suggest writing them a letter via postal mail, but nowadays you can also dispute charges online. The problem with filing a dispute online is that oftentimes, you agree to not being able to sue them if the charge is not removed. You limit your rights, giving you less control and making the process less effective.

Also, do not dispute via phone. You need evidence and records of your dispute. You can easily find a sample letter which you can send to the credit bureaus. All the credit bureaus also have their own dispute letter form, just check their website. Print and mail the dispute letter along with ID and proof of address.

Step 4: Passed Payment History

Your past payment history has the biggest impact. Fix any late payments and avoid late payments in the future. What you can do is setting up payment due alerts and becoming more organized. If the due dates are inconsistent with the dates you get paid, talk with your bank or lender to change the payment date. If you get paid at the end of every month, change your due date to the end of every month too. If fixing any late payments is hard, request the issuer or lender if they can forgive the charge. Tell them that you were out on vacation, the check got lost via the mail, or you did not get notice of the bill and did not know it existed. Some issuers, especially credit card issuers, are pretty soft-hearted if you have had a strong track record of making payments in the past. What is worse than having a bad payment history, is having no payment history. If you have no payment history, try getting a secured credit card and making on-time payments in order to build up a healthy payment history. Really try to pay your bills on time in the future.

Step 5: Debt-to-Credit Ratio

Keep the balances low. Avoid maxing out. You could make all your payments on time, but it is also essential to keep your balance low when it comes to your credit card, or any revolving credit account for that matter. Credit cards are the main weight of debt-ratio rates, so if you do not have a credit card, definitely get one. To figure out your credit card's debt-ratio, divide your credit card balance by your available credit line. So if you spent $200 out of your $1000 credit line, that's 200/1000=0.2, which is 20%. This is good. FICO recommends a debt-to-credit ratio to be under 30%. If your debt-to-credit ratio is at or above 30%, decrease your spending or increase your credit line, your bank will likely agree to increasing your credit line.

Step 6: Negotiate your existing accounts

If you have open accounts that are severely delinquent, showing late payments or slow payments contact the creditor(s) and try to negotiate a new payment arrangement.

- Ask for more time to pay-off the loan; consider this, if you have a 36 months term loan ask if it can be extended to 42 months
- Ask for a lower interest rate?
- Ask what are your options?
- You can do this yourself without the help of those companies and organizations that try to put you on a special payment plan charging lots of money to do something you can do for yourself. This is extra money that can be used to pay off some of that

debt. Simply explain to the creditor(s) you are having financial difficulties, below are some typical hardships:

- going through a divorce
- getting sick and being under-insured or no medical insurance
- death of a close relative (parent, sibling, spouse, child)
- losing a job or job cutting back on hours
- a major car repairs (replace engine/transmission)
- car accident
- becoming disabled
- a run of bad luck, etcetera

Remember to notate your schedule on all the progress you have made negotiating your payoffs.

Chapter 3. Strategies to Repair your Credit Score

Pay to Delete Strategy

If you have derogatory items in your credit report, you can opt to pay the unpaid credit balance only if the creditor agrees to delete the items from your credit report. As I already mentioned, don't agree for a $0 balance appearing on your credit report since this taints your reputation. This will ultimately improve your rating. Actually, the idea is to ensure that whatever amount you agree to pay doesn't show up as your last date of activity. If the creditor only cares about their money, why should they bother telling the world that you have finally paid?

In most instances, the creditors often write off debts within just 2 years of constant defaulting after which this information is sold in bulk to a collection company for some pennies of a dollar. This means that the collection companies will even be just fine if you even pay a fraction of what you ought to pay. Whatever you pay, they will still make money! This makes them open to negotiations such as pay to delete since they have nothing to lose anyway.

Chapter 1. Therefore, only use the pay to delete approach at this level and not any other. Actually, the only other way around it for the collection company is a judgment, which can be costly, so you have some advantage here.

Chapter 2. Additionally, use this strategy when new negative items start showing up in your report that could hurt your reputation as a credit consumer.

Chapter 3. Also, since the creditors will often sell the same information to multiple collection companies, you might probably start noting the same debt being reported by several companies; use pay to delete to get them off your report.

Chapter 4. You can also use this strategy if you have not been successful in getting items off your credit report using other methods. This is opting to go the dispute way might only make the process cyclic, which will be cumbersome, tiresome and frustrating; you don't want to get into this cycle.

Now that you know when to use this method, understanding how the entire process works is very critical. To start with, ensure that you get an acceptance in writing if they agree to your times; don't pay without the letter! After you agree, allow about 45 days for next credit report to be availed to you by your credit monitoring service. These companies have the legal power to initiate the deletion process so don't accept anything less such as updating the balance; it is either a deletion or nothing. Don't worry if one company seems not to agree with your terms since another one will probably show up and will gladly take the offer.

In any case, what do they have to gain when they keep your debt when you are willing to pay? Remember that the records will just be in your records for 7 years so since 2 years are already past, these companies have no choice otherwise you can simply let the 7 years to pass! However, don't use this as an excuse for not paying your debts since the creditors can sue you to compel you to pay outstanding amounts. The aim of this process is to ensure that whatever bad experience you have with one creditor doesn't make the others to make unfavorable decisions on your part.

NOTE: don't be overly aggressive with creditors who have a lot to lose in the process especially the recent creditors since they can probably sue you. Your goal is to only be aggressive with creditors that are barred by the statute of limitation from suing you in court. You don't want to find yourself in legal trouble to add to your existing problems. Try and remain as smart as possible and make all the right moves to help you repair your credit at the earliest.

Pay to delete isn't the only option available to you; you can use other strategies to repair your credit.

Check for FDCPA (Fair Debt Collection Practices Act) Violations

The law is very clear on what collection agencies can do

and what they cannot do as far as debt collection is concerned. For instance:

- They should not call you more than once in a day unless they can prove that it was accidentally dialed by their automated systems.
- They cannot call you before 8.00.am or after 9.00pm.
- They cannot threaten, belittle or yell at you to make you pay any outstanding debts.
- They cannot tell anyone else other than your spouse why they are contacting you.

- The best way to go about this is to let them know that you are recording all their calls.
- They cannot take more money from your account than you have authorized if they do an ACH.
- They are also not allowed to send you collection letters if you have already sent them a cease and desist order.

If you can prove that collection companies are in violation of the laws, you should file a complaint with the company then have your lawyer send proof indicating the violations; you can then request that any outstanding debt be forgiven. You need to understand that the law is on your side in such circumstances; actually, if the violations are major, the collection companies could be forced to pay fines of up to $10,000 for these violations.

So, if your debt is significantly lower than this, you could be on your way to having your debt cleared since these companies would rather pay your debt than pay the fine. Look for Errors on your Credit Reports

Your credit report should be free of errors. Even the slightest thing as reporting the wrong date of last activity on your credit report is enough to damage your credit. If the write off date is different from what has been reported, you can dispute the entry to have it corrected to reflect that actual status of your credit. However, keep in mind that the credit bureaus will in most instances confirm that the negative entry is correct even if this is not the case, which means that they will not remove the erroneous item.

You must put in efforts to get them on the right track. To get them to comply, you have to inform them that the law requires them to have preponderance of their systems in place to ensure that these errors do not arise. Therefore, the mere fact of confirming the initial error is not enough. Inform them about the Notice (Summons) and complaint to let them understand that you are serious about the matter. Once they have an idea of your stance, they will put in efforts to do the right thing. The thing is; the bureaus don't want any case to go to court since this could ultimately provide proof that their systems are weak or flawed, which means that they will probably be in some bigger problems.

So try and drive a strong point across so that they understand you mean business. Mere exchange of emails will not do and you must send them details on how strong your case will be. This will make them understand their position and they will decide to help you to avoid going to court. This will, in turn, work to your advantage in making them to dig deeper into the issue. However, this method will only work if you are certain that an error was actually made. You will also require proof for it and cannot simply state that there was an error.

Request Proof of the Original Debt

If you are certain that the credit card has been written off for late payment, it is highly likely that the carriers (Capital One and Citibank) cannot find the original billing statements within 30 days, which  they are required by the law to respond. This in effect allows you to have whatever entry you have disputed removed from the credit report as if it never happened.

Another handy approach is to request for the original contract that you signed to be provided to prove that you actually opened that particular credit card in the first instance. As you do this, don't just ask for "verification" since this just prompts the collection agency to "verify" that they actually received a request for collection on an account that has your name on it. Pay the Original Creditor

When your debt is sold to collection agencies, you will probably risk having new items showing up on your credit report, which can further hurt your credit rating. However, you can stop that by sending a check with the full payment of any outstanding amount to the original creditor after which you just send a proof of payment to that collection agency and any other then request them to delete any derogatory items they have reported from your credit report.

It is always a good idea to be in direct contact with your creditor or creditors. In fact, many of these agencies will be fully equipped to cheat you and will follow through on plans to have your report show bad credit scores. It is up to you to try and remove these "middlemen" and do the payment yourself. You could also enter into an agreement to pay a portion of the money to the creditor as full payment for the sum (the pay to delete strategy).

Under the federal law, if the original creditor accepts any payment as full payment for any outstanding debt, the collection agency has to remove whatever they have reported. This will only work if the original creditor accepts the payment; it is possible for some of the checks you pay to the original creditor to be returned to you.

How to remove your Debt

Remember that you need to focus on paying off all your debts at the earliest. You cannot waste any more time and must try and finish them off to have a good score. Let us now look at the things that you need to do to pay off your debts on time.

You can pay off your debts in one of the two methods that are made available viz. the first one being the avalanche method and the second being the snowball method. Each type has its own advantages and disadvantages. You need to look at whatever fits your budget best and go for it without wasting any more time. If you think you have enough money saved up then choose the avalanche method but if you have very little then chose the snowballing method. Apart from these, if you have enough money to pay everything all together then you can choose that option as well.

Planning

Remember to always work with a plan. When you have everything planned out it will be easy for you to finish your task. Start by preparing a monthly budget by including your incomes and expenses and try and balance it out to remain with as much money at the end as possible. You need to add your debts to the expenses column and this will help you pay them on time. When you are left with a surplus, you can use it to open a separate "debt repayment" account and add in the money there. Once you have a substantial amount, you can use it to pay off all your debts.

Organizing

Mere planning will not suffice and you need to be as organized as possible. You must have everything in place to help you operate smoothly. Try having a different account for each of your debts so that money automatically gets transferred every month. You must also have a set monthly budget for your expenses. You must not use any more money than what you have assigned. When you are organized, you will feel that your life is easy and there are not many obstacles standing in your way.

Contact

The next step is to contact your creditors. This means that you get in touch with them and assure them that you are going to pay your debts on time. Many times, it pays to develop a good rapport with your creditors. But don't push it and remain within your limits. You need to develop a rapport and not a close friendship with them. You need to win over their trust and make them like your determination. Remain in touch with them and update them on your every move to repay their debts on time. After a while, the informality between the two of you will start to reduce.

Negotiate

When you have struck a good rapport, you can decide to ask for a small rebate in your debt or negotiate the rate of interest that you have to pay. This might not be possible with all creditors such as banks but you can try your luck with moneylenders and other non-commercial lenders. Once they are happy with your timely debt repayments they might decide to reduce the interest rate by a little. But don't expect them to waive off your loan as nobody will be willing to do that. You can ask them if you can pay a little less for the last few installments and count that as your rebate.

Secured credit card

When you are trying to pay off all your debts at the earliest, you must not use your credit card excessively. Your credit score will plummet and so, it is best that you give up on these. There are alternatives to credit cards that you can consider. Debit cards are a great idea as you will only draw money from your own account when you use these. Buy if you want to have the feel of a credit card then you can opt for a secured credit card. These are issued by your bank and they will be linked to your account. You will have to add money to this account and there will be a limit on how much you can draw in a month. There will be no interest levied on the amount and you must add back the money that you withdrew within a specified period of time to help the account remain active.

Family

Sometimes, if there is a lot of debt then you can consider borrowing some money from your relatives. When you do so, you will be able to pay off a debt easily. Your family members might not charge you a high rate of interest and it might be within your budget. You can consider asking your dad or your uncle or anybody who is in a position to pay you the amount at the earliest. You need not stress over paying the sum back to them and can do it leisurely and at your own pace.

Life insurance

It is also possible for you to borrow money from your life insurance policy. You can ask for a certain amount that you promise to pay back within a specified period of time. There is no interest as such that will be levied on this sum and you can repay it after a few years' time. Once you repay your debt and give back to your insurance company then you will truly be free and your credit score will start to rise high.

Bank borrowing

It pays to have everything unified to make for easy payments. This means that you can borrow a certain amount from your bank and pay off all

your creditors in bulk. You can then pay only to your bank to settle your debts. This will make it easier for you as you have to pay to only one institution. The rate of interest might also be low and that will help you save on a lot of money. The only disadvantage of this type is that, not many banks entertain this sort of borrowing. However, you can try your luck and approach two or more banks with a proposal.

Money savers

Every month, think of ways in which you can save on money. This can be by way of using coupons while shopping or making use of store credit to help save on the bill etc. You can also sell your old and unused stuff to make some money out of it. It is also a good idea to gift a service instead of a physical gift as this will further help you in saving money. Nevertheless, if you cannot gift a service every time then you can consider buying them in bulk after the holiday is over and store it to be gifted the next year. Cutting down on electricity, water and gas bills will also help you save money. It is also ideal for you to buy second hand goods for the time being and save further.

You can follow these steps to repay all your loans at the earliest and improve your credit score.

Chapter 4. Understanding FCRA and Section 609

When you are going about trying to fix your credit, it can often feel as though the deck is stacked against you, however, the truth of the matter is that there are several laws that can help you to even the odds when it comes to dealing with both creditors and credit bureaus.

FCRA: The FCRA does more than just provide you with a free credit report each year, it also regulates the various credit reporting organizations and helps to ensure that the information they gather on you is both accurate and fair. This means that if you see inaccurate information on your credit report, and report it to the relevant agency, they are legally required to look into the matter and resolve it, typically within 30 days. The same applies to agencies or organizations that generally add details to your credit report. Finally, if an organization that reviews your credit report decides to charge your more or declines to do business with you based on what they find in your report, they are legally obligated to let you know why and what report they found the negative information in.

While this won't help you with that particular lender, if the information is inaccurate you will at least know where to go to clear up the issue. Additionally, if

you report an inaccuracy and the credit reporting agency ignores your request you can sue them to recover the damages or a minimum of $2,500. You may also be able to win an additional amount based on punitive damages and legal fees and any other associated costs. You must file legal proceedings within 5 years of when this occurs.

What Is Section 609? Is a 609 Dispute Letter Effective?

The first thing that we need to take a look at here when it comes to our credit scores is what Section 609 is really all about. This is going to be one of the best ways for you to get your credit score up, and outside of a little calling or sending out mail, you will not have to do as much to get it all done. Let's dive in now and see if we are able to learn a bit more about it.

The FCRA or the Fair Credit Reporting Act, is going to cover a lot of the aspects and the components of credit checking to make sure that it is able to maintain a reasonable amount of privacy and accuracy along the way. This agency is going to list out all of the responsibilities that credit reporting companies, and any credit bureaus, will have, and it also includes the rights of the consumer, which will be your rights in this situation. This Act is going to be the part that will govern how everything is going to work to ensure that all parties are treated in a fair manner.

This Act is going to limit the access that third-parties can have to your file. You personally have to go through and provide your consent before someone is able to go through and look at your credit score, whether it is a potential employer or another institution providing you with funding.

They are not able to get in and just look at it. Keep in mind that if you do not agree for them to take a look at the information, it is going to likely result in you not getting the funding that you want, because there are very few ways that the institution can fairly assess the risk that you pose to them in terms of creditworthiness.

There are several ways that a credit agency can go through and break or violate the FCRA, so this allows the consumer a way to protect themselves if that proves to be something that needs to happen.

Another thing to note about all of this is that the FCRA is going to be divided into sections. In particular, section 609 of the FCRA is going to deal with disclosure and is going to put all of the burdens of providing the right kind of documentation on the credit bureaus.

This may sound a little bit confusing, but it means that you may have debt or another negative item that is on your credit report, but there is a way to get around this without having to wait for years to get that to drop off your report or having to pay back a debt that you are not able to afford.

Keep in mind that this is not meant to be a method for you to take on a lot of debts that you can't afford and then just dump them. But on occasion, there could be a few that you are able to fight and get an instant boost to your credit score in the process.

You do not have to come up with a way of proving whether or not the item on the credit report is legitimate or not. Instead, that is up to the credit bureaus. And there are many cases where they are not able to do this. Whether they bought the debt and did not have the proper documentation, or there is something else that is wrong with it, the credit company may not be able to prove that you are the owner of it or that you owe on it at all. If this is the case, they have to remove the information from your credit report. When a bad debt is taken off, or even a collection is taken off, that does nothing but a lot of good for your overall score.

Some of Your Rights Under Section 609 and How You Can Use These to Your Advantage.

According to Section 609 of the Fair Credit Reporting Act, the credit bureaus are not allowed to list any credit agreements without verifying their validity first. The creditor is supposed to send a copy of the credit agreement for the bureaus to validate and keep in case there are any inquiries.

This is important because the bureaus generally skip this step. It is expensive and time consuming for them to verify all the information they receive. By law, the bureaus are required to provide proof that they have verified the information within thirty days. If they cannot provide proof of the original agreement or subsequent evidence of negative listings, and you can prove your identity, then they must remove the listing. It does not matter if the information is accurate or not. That is why it's important to monitor your credit.

To take advantage of this law, the first thing you need to do is to send a physical letter to the billing inquiries address that the creditor provides. If they turn down your request you are then allowed to ask for all the documentation saying why they turned you down.

A subset of this law is what is known as the Hidden Gem Law, this means you can

dispute any transaction made within 100 miles of your home, or anywhere in your home state, which exceeds $50. If the debt collector breaks these rules or acts in other ways they are not allowed then you can file a private lawsuit and be recouped costs, fees and damages. What's more, you don't even need to prove damages and you will likely be awarded a minimum of $1,000.

Ways to Approach the Financial Institution

If the credit reporting agency is struggling to alter your report and you think the information is incomplete or wrong --you will want to take action. Below are a few suggestions that will assist you with your attempts.

Contact the Creditor Directly

Contacts the lender, which supplied the advice and demand it inform the credit. Request to Creditor composes your letter or to Eliminate. You can use inaccurate Information. You receive a letter from the lender and ought to be deleted from the credit history if, send a copy of the letter to the bureau that made the faulty report. If you contacted the Funding, it does not need to manage this dispute unless you supply the info. But since you think you also demonstrate a foundation for the belief, and the dispute wasn't properly researched should you increase your complaint, just like the president or CEO, the provider is very likely to reply. If the company cannot or won't help you in removing the info that is inaccurate, call the credit reporting agency.

Document another Dispute with the Credit Reporting Agency with More Information

If you have info backs up your claim, it is possible to submit a fresh dispute. Make sure to provide info. Should you dispute the mistake without giving any info to the bureau, it will determine that your dispute is frivolous, so the bureau does not need to inquire into the issue.

File a Complaint about the Credit Reporting Agency

Letter #1

(Initial Letter to Credit Bureau Disputing Items)

{Name of Bureau}

{Address}

{Date}

{Name on account}

{Report number}

To whom it may concern:

On {Date of Credit Report} I received a copy of my credit report which contains errors that are damaging to my credit score. I am requesting the following items be completely investigated as each account contains several mistakes.

{Creditor 1 / Account number}

{Creditor 2 / Account number}

{Creditor 3 / Account number}

Thank you in advance for your time. I understand that you need to check with the original creditors on these accounts and that you will make sure every detail is accurate. I also understand that under the Fair Credit Reporting Act you will need to complete your investigation within 30 days of receiving this letter. Once you are finished with your investigation, please send me a copy of my new credit report showing the changes. Looking forward to hear from you as I am actively looking for a new job and wouldn't want these mistakes on my credit report to stand in my way.

Sincerely,

{Your signature}

{Your Printed Name}

{Your Address}

{Your Phone Number}

{Your Social Security Number}

Attach a copy of the credit report showing which accounts you are disputing

Letter #2

(When you don't get a response from Letter #1)

{Name of Bureau}

{Address}

{Date}

{Name on account}

{Report number}

To whom it may concern:

On {Date of your first letter} I sent you a letter asking you to investigate several mistakes on my credit report. I've included a copy of my first letter and a copy of the report with the mistakes circled. The Fair Credit Reporting Act says I should only have to wait 30 days for the investigation to be finished. It has been more than 30 days and I still have not heard anything.

I'm guessing that since you have not responded that you were not able to verify the information on the mistaken accounts. Since it has been more than 30 days, please remove the mistakes from my credit report and send me a copy of my updated credit report. Also, as required by law, please send an updated copy of my credit report to anyone who requested a copy of my credit file in the past six months.

Looking forward to hear from you as I am actively looking for a new job and wouldn't want these mistakes on my credit report to stand in my way.

Sincerely,

{Your signature}

{Your Printed Name}

{Your Address}

{Your Phone Number}

{Your Social Security Number}

Attach a copy of the credit report showing which accounts you are disputing

Attach a copy of your original letter

Attach a copy of the registered letter receipts showing the date they received your original letter

Letter #3

(Request for removal of negative items from original creditor)

{Name of Creditor}

{Address}

{Date}

{Name on account}

To whom it may concern:

On {Date of Credit Report} I received a copy of my credit report which contains errors that are damaging to my credit score. I am requesting the following items be completely investigated as each account contains several mistakes.

{Description of item(s) you are disputing/account number(s)}

I have enclosed a duplicate of the credit report and have highlighted the account(s) in question.

Thank you in advance for your time. I understand that you need to check on these accounts and that you will make sure every detail is accurate. I also understand that under the Fair Credit Reporting Act you will need to complete your investigation within 30 days of receiving this letter. Once you are finished with your investigation, please alert all major credit bureaus where you have reported my information. Also, please send me a letter confirming the changes.

Looking forward to hear from you as I am actively looking for a new job and wouldn't want these mistakes on my credit report to stand in my way.

Sincerely,

{Your signature}

{Your Printed Name}

{Your Address}

{Your Phone Number}

{Your Social Security Number}

Attach a copy of the credit report showing which accounts you are disputing

Letter #4

(If you don't receive a response from Letter #3)

{Name of Creditor}

{Address}

{Date}

{Name on account}

To whom it may concern:

On {Date of your first letter} I sent you a letter asking you to investigate several mistakes on my credit report. I've included a copy of my first letter and a copy of the report with the mistakes circled. The Fair Credit Reporting Act says I should only have to wait 30 days for the investigation to be finished. It has been more than 30 days and I still have not heard anything.

I'm guessing that since you have not responded that you were not able to verify the information on the mistaken accounts. Since it has been more than 30 days, please immediately report the updated information to all major credit bureaus so they may update my credit report. Also, please send me a letter confirming these changes to the way you report my account.

Looking forward to hear from you as I am actively looking for a new job and wouldn't want these mistakes on my credit report to stand in my way.

Sincerely,

{Your signature}

{Your Printed Name}

{Your Address}

{Your Phone Number}

{Your Social Security Number}

Attach a copy of the credit report showing which accounts you are disputing

Attach a copy of your original letter

Attach a copy of the registered letter receipts showing the date they received your original letter

Letter #5

(If the Credit Bureau doesn't remove negative items disputed)

{Name of Credit Bureau}

{Address}

{Date}

{Name on account}

{Report number}

To whom it may concern:

On {Date of your first letter} I sent you a letter asking you to investigate several mistakes on my credit report. I've included a copy of my first letter and a copy of the report with the mistakes circled. According to your response you have chosen to leave these negative items on my credit report adding insult to injury. The items in question are:

{Creditor 1 / Account number}

{Creditor 2 / Account number}

{Creditor 3 / Account number}

I find it completely unacceptable that you and the creditor refuse to properly investigate my dispute. Your refusal to follow the Fair Credit Reporting Act is causing me untold stress and anxiety. Since you won't follow through, I want to know exactly how you investigated each account. Therefore, I would like the name, title and contact information for the person at the creditor with whom you did the investigation. This will let me personally follow up with the creditor and find out why they are choosing to report these mistakes on my credit month after month.

I see I am only one person among thousands or more that you have to look after, but to me this is both personally damaging and humiliating. You may not understand it and you don't have to--all I'm asking is that when people look at my credit file, they see the most accurate information and that's not what's happening.

Please provide me with the requested information right away so I can finally put this nightmare behind me.

Looking forward to hear from you as I am actively looking for a new job and wouldn't want these mistakes on my credit report to stand in my way.

Sincerely,

{Your signature}

{Your Printed Name}

{Your Address}

{Your Phone Number}

{Your Social Security Number}

Attach a copy of the credit report showing which accounts you are disputing

Attach a copy of your original letter

Attach a copy of the Bureau's response showing no changes to your credit

Goodwill Letter

A Goodwill letter is a request you make to a creditor based on your past and future relationship. Below is an example of a goodwill letter you can use:

Date:

Name of Credit Bureau

Address of Credit Bureau

City, State, Zip

To Whom It May Concern:

I am writing this letter in hope of getting some assistance with my account number. I am hoping to have an adjustment made out of "Goodwill" on my credit report regarding the late payments that were made on this account. I take full responsibility for my actions. At the time of the late payments I was experiencing a financial hardship and since then I have been consistent with my payment obligations with the company.

I am a loyal satisfied customer with the company and will continue to be long into the future. Based on my past and current payment history it shows that outside of this time period I have always made my payments on time. I would greatly appreciate it if you would consider removing the negative marking that are being report to the credit bureaus. I look forward to hearing back from you as soon as you have made your decision. Thank you so much for your attention to this matter at it is of great importance to me.

Sincerely,

Name:

Address:

Phone number:

If the good will letter fails, then you can try disputing.

Hardship Letter

Think of a hardship letter as an extreme goodwill letter. This letter is used when you have several late payments or are behind on payments and can bring the account current.

In essence, you are asking for a little compassion. Terrible things happen all the time but we all need a break now and again.

Here is a sample letter:

Dear [creditor],

I have recently suffered a serious financial hardship when {spouse died, medical emergency, job loss, business failure, natural disaster... describe the hardship here in moderate detail.}

As a result of this hardship, I have fallen behind on my account with you and would like to do what I can to remedy the situation.

I have {x} late payments on my credit report as a result of this. I am writing to ask, as a matter of good faith, if you would remove the late payments on this account if I can bring the account current and pay all associated late fees.

I would like to salvage my credit and my relationship with you as a creditor as I've been a loyal customer for {x} years!

Any help you can provide or any other options you may have are very much appreciated.

Sincerely,

Customer

While we tend to think of lenders as big uncompassionate machines we need to remember that there are caring and feeling people running those machines.

People can be reasoned with provided you have a real hardship.

Besides, lenders don't make money by sending your account to collections. You just have to give them a reason to work with you and you might be surprised by the results.

Chapter 6. Consequences of Not Paying off Your Debt

What happens when you go into serious delinquency or default on your loans? Well, it depends on the type of loan. With cars and houses, they can be repossessed by the bank. With  consumer debt, you are often going to have to declare bankruptcy to wipe out old debts if you are far enough underwater.

Government-backed student loans, however, are a whole different beast. They can NOT be removed via bankruptcy. After 270 days of no payments, they are officially in default and sit there like a bad acne breakout on your credit report, making your score look yucky. Some student loan companies will then turn the loans over to official debt collection companies, which start yammering your phone away about late payments. In addition, you'll be on the hook for their own special fees. Yay.

You might have to try the 'secured credit card' trick to build up your credit again after this kind of financial disaster. Some people want to reach out to a debt settlement company or try to get a payday loan, but please don't! Debt settlement companies have to get paid too, you know, and they'll come after your money one way or another. Most of them are scams. The only honest ones are nonprofits, and even those are doubtful. Payday loans charge sickening interest rates of more than 500% in some cases, so for a $1,000 payday loan, you'll be screwed out of more than $5,000. What kind of sense does that make? Stay far away from them.

If you don't pay your credit cards, they sit untouched with the original creditor for about six months. An original creditor is a bank like Chase, Citi, Capital One, Discover, or American Express. If you keep making payments, even if it's just $10 a month, the account will remain open with the original creditor.

But if you stop making payments for six months, then the original creditor turns the debt along with its collected interest over to a debt collection company. They then attempt to collect the debt for another six months. By now, you've not made a single payment for a year. If no payments are made, then your debt, with any added fees and other expenses from the debt collection company, is then turned over to a law office, where a judgment is brought against you in the form of a lawsuit. The law office represents either the original creditor or the debt buying company. The amount of small claims lawsuits based on collecting past debts has increased significantly in the past ten years, and now there are specialty law firms devoted solely to debt collecting from average people. Well, at least we don't have debtors' prisons anymore.

If this happens, the creditor or debt collector is the plaintiff, and you become the defendant. You can even go to trial and meet with a lawyer to set up court-ordered payment plans based on your actual financial paperwork that you bring to the courthouse. Keep in mind that there is often interest included even after judgment is brought against you.

If you still fail to pay, a lien could be put on your property and your wages could be garnished from your current paycheck. It's legal in most states to garnish up to 25% of your wages. However, if you are seriously buried, you should know that the great state of Texas does not allow wage garnishment so if you are considering a move, Texas might be the place!

Being informed about this entire process will help you make better decisions on repairing your credit before bills go to collections. Dealing with debt collectors is its own game, so let's take a look. It's a bit different than just dealing with a credit card company. The rules have changed.

Make Debt Collectors Go Away

Unfortunately, debt collector companies just won't take your word for it that you're going through a rough time or that they need to leave you alone. They do need to see proof. Collectors love paperwork! The more proof in writing, the better. So, before calling up your debt collector to give them the complete story of why you can't pay, get yourself prepared.

Spend the time gathering up all of your financial paperwork. Get copies of your taxes that show your income and your financial situation. Gather your  doctor's bills, your SSDI paperwork, your paystubs, and, if you're sharing an income or living on someone else's SSI, all the paperwork that goes along with that person.

Then, once you've gathered all your paperwork, call up your collector. Keep an eye on the prompts on the phone until you get to the customer service department. Be prepared to wait a long time on the phone. Just set aside the time to devote to this. Be polite, but brief and direct. Tell the representative that you can't pay and you have the proof you can't. Ask them how you can get them the paperwork so they can attach it to your file. Maybe you can send it in an email as a PDF attachment or mail it or fax it to them? Get the name of the representative and the state (or country) where they are. Take down your account number. Ask if you need to provide any other paperwork as proof of the inability to pay. If they tell you that you need something, comply with that. Ask if they can put a financial hardship status on your account. If so, that's great. Many collectors don't.

After you hang up, immediately follow the representative's instructions to send the paperwork to the collector. Keep all originals and only send copies. After two weeks, call up the customer service department again. Explain that you spoke to "Name" and have they received all of your paperwork? Make sure every last piece of paper is attached to your file.

The third step is to put your name on their "Do Not Call" list. VERY IMPORTANT: Keep in mind that they won't call about important stuff, either, like courtesy calls notifying you that your balance has changed. So, do this with caution. Yes, the phone calls are uber annoying. But, that's the primary legal way of contacting you.

You actually need to send your request to not be contacted in writing. Write or type legibly on a blank sheet of paper:

To Capital One,

Please put my name on your "Do Not Call" list. Please remove my name from all call lists. I understand that I will not receive any phone calls.

Thank you,

Your Name

Keep a copy, in case you need it for legal purposes. After you've mailed your request to the collector, wait three weeks for them to receive it and attach the request to your file. Your account will be flagged "Do Not Call" if it's been done properly. Follow up and call the collector to make sure your account has been flagged. Ask the representative if you need to do anything else to make sure you are not contacted.

Throughout this whole negotiating process, continue to send what payments you can. Yes, you can absolutely send small payments to a debt collector, even if it's just $10 or $20 a month. It buys you a little time to change your financial situation. Don't give up and don't just stop sending payments.

You can also settle with debt collectors. Ask them about settlement options and start with less than 50% of the debt owed. They might come back with a counter-offerIf you do this, make sure you have them put Paid in Full on your credit report if possible.

Make sure the proper paperwork is attached to your file and your address is correct. You'd be surprised at how much incorrect information can get attached to your account.

Repair Credit Solution

By making your financial goals, setting your budget, finding ways to save money, and requesting a copy of your credit report, you've done your preliminary legwork in trying to get your finances back in order.

Now that all three credit reporting agencies have a copy of your credit report, it's time to roll up your sleeves and tackle the inaccurate information reported on your credit report.

Reviewing Your Credit Report

When you check each of your credit reports, whether it is on the website of the credit reporting agency where you can download it, or a hard copy of your report which you received in the mail, it is vital that each entry is accurately reported.

When you consider misleading or incorrect information on the credit report, the Equal Credit Reporting Act notes you have the right to dispute the submission with the credit reporting agency. The credit reporting agency has to re-examine the creditor's admission. The enquiry must be concluded within 30 days of receiving the lawsuit message.

If the borrower fails to respond within that time period, the credit reporting agency must delete from the credit report the entry you are contesting. If the creditor replies and the inaccurate entry are corrected, the credit reporting agency will update your credit report. There is also the risk that the borrower can respond to the credit report and not make any changes in it. If you're not happy with your revised credit report, you should write a 100-word paragraph to clarify your side of the story on any of the remaining items on the credit report. This customer statement will then surface any time it appears on your credit report. If you don't want to write a 100-word paragraph on your credit report, you will be able to write another 120-day appeal letter from your most recent credit report.

When you access your credit report on the Website of the credit reporting agency, you will be able to dispute the incorrect entries online. The site will have boxes to check for inaccuracy alongside an appropriate reason. If you choose to write a personalized message, you can also use the same answers as appropriate. Sample answers would be:

- This is not my account.

- This was not late as indicated.

- This was not charged off.

- This was paid off in full as agreed.

- This was not a collection account.

- This is not my bankruptcy as indicated.

- This is not my tax lien as indicated.

- This is not my judgment as indicated.

What you shouldn't do:

- Alter your identity, or try to change it.

- The story is fictional.

- Check any information which is 100% correct.

What you should do:

- Read your emails, should you decide to send them to us? If a letter looks legitimate, credit reporting agencies will believe it has been written by a credit repair service, and they will not investigate the dispute.

- Use your original letterhead (if you do have one).

- Use the appeal form included with the credit report by the credit reporting agency, if you want.

- Provide some evidence suggesting the wrong entry is erroneous.

- Include the identification number for all communications listed on the credit report.

Common Credit Report Errors

Note, there could be various mistakes in each of the three credit reports. It is not uncommon to have positive coverage of an account on one article, but poor reports on another.

Here are some of the most common credit report errors.

- Listed wrong names, emails, or phone numbers.

- Data that refers to another of the same name.

- Duplicate details, whether positive or negative, about the same account.

- Records have negative, apparently positive information.

- Balances on accounts payable are still on view.

- Delinquent payment reports that were never billed in due time.

- This indicates wrong credit limits.

- Claims included in the insolvency which are still due.

- Incorrect activity dates;

- Past-due payments not payable.

- Court records which are falsely connected with you, such as convictions and bankruptcy.

- Tax liens not yours.

- Unprecedented foreclosures.

Spotting Possible Identity Theft

Checking your credit report could also spot potential identity theft. That's why you should inquire at least once a year or every six months for a copy of your credit report.

Things to look for would be:

- Names of accounts and figures that you do not know.

- You don't remember filling out loan applications.

- Addresses you didn't live in.

- Poor bosses or tenants enquiries you don't know.

Creditors Can Help

Many times, if you have had a long-term account with a creditor, you can contact them directly and explain the error being reported on your credit report.

Ask them to write you a letter with the email and correction. Also ask them to contact every credit reporting agency that reports this incorrect entry in order to make the correction.

Once the creditor receives a copy of the letter, make a copy of it and attach the letter to the letter of dispute you send. Mail it to the agency for credit reporting, and ask them to update their files. Once that is completed, you will be sent back a new credit report by the credit reporting agency.

Credit Rescoring

Rapid rescoring is an expedited way of fixing anomalies in the credit file of a customer. The bad news is, you can't do it yourself. A fast rescore dispute process works through

borrowers and mortgage brokers, a number of approved registry credit reporting companies, and credit reporting agencies.

If you are a creditor applying for a rescore on your credit report, you would need to provide detailed documents that would be sent to the collateral agencies that are working on your case. Cash registry is the system used by cash grantors. The data archive gathers the records from the three main credit reporting agencies, and has to check the consumer's initial information for a rescore. Once the verification is entered into the program of the repository a new score will be produced.

The key thing to keep in mind is that a simple rescore can only be temporary. You may be able to close a loan with it, but you must follow through on your credit report with the three main credit reporting firms to ensure it has been removed or corrected. If it reappears, forward the reports immediately to credit reporting agencies.

The downside of a fast rescore is that you save money without having to contend individually with a credit reporting agency that may take longer than 30 days to complete an audit. If the sale of a house or lease depends on your credit score, and you're in a time crunch, the best solution is to easily rescore.

Should You Use a Credit Repair Company?

Using a credit repair company's services is basically hiring a firm to do what you can do for yourself. The process is really without secrets. All the credit repair company does is dispute information on negative entries on your credit report with credit reporting agencies. Most companies may report having agreements with credit reporting agencies or have a secret way to get borrowers to delete unfavorable entries. This is more than likely not true because both state and federal laws under the Fair Credit Reporting Act regulate the credit reporting agencies.

You will be charged a fee for working with a credit repair company. Many systems will call up your credit records or allow you to access your own reports. The letter-writing campaign starts after you have entered into a contract with the firm.

The reason some people hire an outsourced credit repair company is because they feel intimidated or have no time to do the work themselves. Until signing up with a credit repair company there are many steps you need to take. Many businesses operate illegally and you don't want to get caught in that trap.

Beware of Credit Repair Scams

Sadly, it is easy for people to fall prey to credit repair fraud when they are vulnerable and are going through financial challenges. If you're looking for a repair company for cash, here's how to say if it's a genuine or scam business. Many scam firms may only sign up to take the money and run for their services. This is a list of stuff that should raise a red flag.

The company wants you to pay for credit repair services before it provides any services.

- The company doesn't tell you your rights, and you can do it for free. This should appear in any document it presents you with.
- The firm advises that you do not explicitly approach any of the three major national credit reporting agencies. It knows that if you do, you may learn that it took your money, and that it does nothing.
- The company tells you that even if that information is accurate, it can get rid of all the negative credit reports in your credit report. No one can promise just one thing on your credit report for change.
- The company assumes you're trying to create a "different" credit identifier. This is known as file segregation. It is accomplished by filing for the use of an Employer Identification Number to create a new credit report instead of the Social Security number. That is utterly unconstitutional.
- The firm encourages you to challenge any information contained in your credit report regardless of accuracy or timeliness of the material. If the evidence is 100% right, then you have no basis for a disagreement.

Remember, if you are given unlawful advice and follow it knowing it is illegal, you may be committing fraud, and you will find yourself in lawful hot water.

If you use the postal, mobile, or Internet to apply for credit and provide false information, you could be charged and prosecuted with mail or wire fraud. Most of the programs you sign on have a promise that the details you receive are valid when signing the contract.

The Credit Service Organizations Act

Credit repair facilities are governed under State and Federal law by the Credit Service Organizations Act. Under this act, most states require  that credit repair companies in each state where they do business be registered and bonded. There are different requirements for each Country. When signing up for this program you will check a copy of your state's Credit Service Organizations Act. The Federal Trade Commission and the offices of the State Attorney General are going after credit repair companies that do not comply with the regulations and are soliciting customers with misleading information. Through visiting:

www.ftc.gov, you can also get a copy of the state edition of the Credit Service Organizations Act.

Some of this law's key provisions are for consumer protection by signing up with a credit repair service. A credit repair company must give you a written contract that outlines your rights and obligations that its state has approved. Make sure to read the paperwork before signing something. So know that a credit repair company can't:

• Make false claims about its facilities, before signing.

• Charge yourself until the promised services are complete.

• Provide certain activities until a formal contract has been signed and a three-day waiting period has been fulfilled. You will cancel the contract during this period, without paying any fees.

Chapter 7. How to Proceed with the Letters

Before we get started here, there are a few tips and rules that we need to follow in order to make sure that we are going to get the most out of the templates that we want to use. We are going to take a look at a number of different letters and templates that we are able to send out to the agencies that report our credit so that we can dispute some of the debt or the negative items that are on our reports. These templates will help you compose and keep your dispute as organized as possible. When you pay attention to some of the details that are there, you are going to find that it is easier to come up with a letter that is convincing and effective.

There are a few different ways that we are able to make sure these letters get back to the right parties, and we are going to take a look at all of them below:

Emails

Our world seems to run online all the time and finding ways to work on our credit scores and not have to waste a lot of time copying things or worrying about the paper trails can seem like a great idea. And in some cases, we may find that sending in our 609 letters through email is going to be the best situation for our needs.

Before you do this, though, make sure that you take the time and do the proper research. You want the forms to end up in the right locations, rather than getting sent to the wrong departments, and not doing anything for you in the process. Most of the time there will be listings for the various departments that you want to handle and work with for each credit agency, so take a look at those.

Again, when you are ready, you need to have as many

details ready to go for this as possible. Just sending in a few lines about the process and thinking that will get things done is foolish. Write out a letter just like you would if you planned to send these by mail and use that as the main body of your email. Mention Section 609 and some of the disputes that you want to bring up.

In addition to this, you need to take some time adding in the other details. Attach some ways to prove your identity to the email, along with a copy of the credit report that has been highlighted to show what is going on and what you would like to dispute. Add in any of the other documentation that is needed to help support your case, and have it as clean and organized as possible to make sure the right people can find it and will utilize this information to help you out.

Doing it All Online

Many of the credit agencies have made it easier to go through and work on some of these claims online. This helps you out because you will not need to go through and print it all off or worry about finding the paperwork or printing a bunch of things off. And if you are already on your credit report, your identification has been taken care of.

Since so many people are online these days, doing this right from the credit report is a simple and easy process to work with, and you will catch onto it fairly quickly. Do not take the easy way out with this. If you just click on the part that you think is wrong and submit a claim on it, this is not enough. There will not be any reference back to Section 609, and you will not be able to get them to necessarily follow the rules that come with Section 609.

This is where being detailed is going to be useful in the long run. When you do submit one of these claims online, make sure that you write a note with it to talk about Section 609, specifically the part of 609 that you want to reference in this dispute. You can usually attach other forms to document who you are and why you think these need to be dropped.

Treat this just like you would if you tried to mail the information to the credit agency. The more details that you are able to include in this, the better. This will help to build up your case and can make it harder for those items to stay on your credit report for a long period of time. Make sure to mention the 30-day time limit as well.

Telephone

A telephone is one method that you can use, but it is not usually the right one for this kind of process. For example, how easy is it going to be to show the credit agency what your driver's license looks like? You can repeat the number over if you would like, but this process is still a bit more laborious than some of the others and does not always work as well as we would hope it could.

However, this is definitely an option that we can use in order to reach the credit agencies, and for some people who are not sure of what their rights are, or would rather talk directly to the individuals in charge about this issue, the telephone can be the right option. Make sure that you have a copy of your credit report in front of you when you start and having some other identification information and more. There is the possibility that the other side is going to have some questions for you, and they will at least want to go through and verify your identity to make sure they are ready to go. But the same rules apply here, and if you do not get a response within 30 days of that phone call, then the information should be erased.

Keep good records of the conversation, who you talked to during that time, what time and date it was, and so on. This will make it easier to get someone to respond to you and can help us to get this to work in our favor. Also, remember that you will need to repeat these phone calls to all three credit bureaus in order to get your information cleared on all of them.

Mail

Another option that you are able to work with is mail. This is usually a good method to use because it allows you a way to send in all of the information at once. Since you probably already have a physical copy of your SSN,

driver's license, the credit report and more, you can get copies of these made pretty quickly, and then send them on with the Section 609 letter that you are working with. This method also allows us a way to go through and circle or highlight the parts of our credit report that we want to point out to the credit reporting agency.

This method is quick and efficient and will make sure that the information gets to the right party. Certified Mail

For the most part, you are going to find that working with certified mail is going to be one of the best options that you can choose. This will ensure that the letter gets to the right place and can tell you for certain when the 30-day countdown is going to begin.

If you send this with regular mail, you have to make some guesses on when the letter will arrive at the end address that you want. And sometimes you will be wrong. If there is a delay in the mailing and it gets there too late, then you may start your 30 days too early. On the other hand, if you assume it is going to take so many days and it takes less, you may wait around too long and miss your chance to take this loophole and use it to your advantage.

Certified mail is able to fix this issue. When the credit agency receives the letter, you will get a receipt about that exact date and even the time. This is going to make it so much easier for you to have exact times, and you can add these to your records. There is no more guessing along the way, and you can be sure that this particular loophole is going to work to your advantage.

Another benefit that comes with certified mail is that you make sure that it gets to its location. If you never get a receipt back or get something back that says the letter was rejected or not left at the right place, then you will know about this ahead of time. On the other hand, if it does get to its location, you will know this and have proof of it.

Sometimes things get lost. If the credit agency says that they did not receive the letter, you will have proof that you sent it and that someone within the business received it and signed for it. Whether the company lost it along the way, or they are trying to be nefarious and not fix the issue for you, the certified mail will help you to get it to all work for you.

When it comes to worrying about those 30 days and how it will affect you, having it all in writing and receipts to show what you have done and when is going to be important. This can take out some of the guesswork in the process and will ensure that you are actually going to get things to work for you if the 30 days have come and gone, and no one will be able to come back and say that you didn't follow the right procedures.

As we can see, there are a few different options that we are able to use when it comes to sending out our Section 609 letters.

Chapter 8. How to Overcome Credit Card Debt

What is a Credit Card Debt?

When you incur a credit card debt, you actually keep borrowing money every month, and that is why it is also known as revolving debt. But it is only good until you have the capacity to repay them but when you can't, the debt keeps accumulating. When compared to the loan accounts, you can actually keep using your credit card accounts for an indefinite period of time. In simpler terms, there is nothing that the company can seize, like a house or a card, even when you have failed to repay them. But yes, if you are not able to repay the money you borrowed from the credit card, it is going to affect your credit score drastically.

How Is Credit Card Debt Accumulated?

When you get a credit card, you will see that there will be a due date within which you have to clear the entire balance that you have accumulated on your credit card, and if you fail to do so, you will be accumulating debt. There is a term called APR or Annual Percentage Rate and this is a rate of interest that is charged on your debt when it keeps accumulating one month after the other. The APR that you will be charged may not be the same with someone else's and this is because it keeps differing with your credit history, the bank issuer, and also the type of card that you have.

The benchmark fed funds rate of the Federal Reserve and the prime rate of the credit card interests is somewhat tied, and that is the average value. The credit card debt will increase or decrease with respect to any changes in the target rate made by the Fed.

Now, I want to give you an even clearer picture of how this debt accumulates. For starters, there is a minimum payment that you will have to pay every month whenever you use your credit card to make purchases. This payment is calculated based on a certain percentage (with some additional interest charges) of your balance. If you pay this amount in full, then well and good, but if you don't, then you will be liable to interest. So, the interest will increase if you pay even lesser. The reason behind this is that the nature of credit card interests is compounding so the interest keeps accruing. Thus, if you take a longer time to clear off the debts, then you will owe a huge amount of money to the company, which is much more than what you actually owed before.

What Happens After 7 Years?

This is basically a time limit until which a record is shown in a credit report. But there are certain other negative issues that will stay in your credit report even after seven years, for example, certain judgments, tax liens that are unpaid, and bankruptcy.

But you also have to keep in mind that if any debt is unpaid, then it is not exactly going to vanish even after seven years. Even if the credit report does not list it, you will still owe that money to the lender.

There are several other legal ways that can be implemented by the lenders, creditors, and debt collectors to collect the debt that you haven't paid. Some of these methods include a court giving permission to garnish your wages, sending letters, calling you, and so on. One thing that you benefit because of this seven-years rule is that when the debt is no longer visible on your credit report, it cannot affect your credit score. Thus, you can actually have a better chance of gaining back a good score. Another thing to keep in mind is that this seven-year term is only for the negative information on your report and not the position information because they will stay on the report forever. You should keep an eye out after the seven- year mark as to whether the credit bureaus have removed that information or not. They usually do it automatically, but in case they don't then you will have to raise a dispute.

Many people have this question of what happens to their debt if they accidentally die. Well, in that case, it will be your estate that will be used to pay the debt off. Remember that the debt will not be shoved in someone else's hand in your family because whatever money you owe, it is your debt and not anyone else's. And so whatever you had, like your accounts and assets will then be used for clearing the debt. And after that, if anything remains from your assets, your heir will receive it.

How to Eliminate Credit Card Debt?
Start Eliminating High-Interest Debts First

When you are trying to eliminate your credit card debt, the biggest obstacle that will stand in your way are the ones that carry a very high rate of interest. Sometimes, the rate of interest can even be in double- digits, sometimes as high as 22%. In that case, paying it off can be a really difficult task. But the reason why I am asking

 you to start eliminating them first because when you will have cleared these debts, you will have a greater amount of money left in your hand at the end of each month.

Another thing that you could do, but only if you have enough credit available, is to apply for a new credit card. But this should be a zero-interest one. Once you get it, transfer the balance to eliminate the high- interest debt. Yes, I know that some of you might be thinking that it is not a sensible thing to do to apply for another credit card and that is why I will be asking you to get it only if you think you have enough self- restraint not to go buy a bunch of stuff that you don't need.

Keep Making Small Payments

Quite contrary to the technique I mentioned above is another technique which is called the snowflake technique. With this process, you will be making small payments towards your debt every time you get some extra cash in hand. Whatever payment you are making, it does not matter as long as you keep paying.

You can pay $10, or you can pay $20 but at the end of the year, you will find that you have reduced about

$1000 simply by paying such small amounts almost every day, even if you are paying $2 on any particular day.

People often ignore this method, thinking that it will be only small amounts but you should not make the mistake of overlooking these small amounts as they have quite the power in them. When you are making these small payments, it would feel as if they are not even leaving any dent but with time, they will sum up and cause a considerable effect on your debt.

Preventive Measures to Avoid Credit Card Debt

Have an Emergency Fund

Think about a situation when you have encountered a problem that requires you to spend a lot of money, for example, a car repair or job loss or medical emergencies. In such a situation, what you need is an emergency fund, but when people don't have that, they resort to credit cards for help.

But why arrive at such a situation when you can build an emergency fund that will cover at least six months' expenses. A fund of this size will help you to figure out any small expenses that crop up overnight. Take your time to build your emergency fund so that you do not have to rely on debt ever.

But Only Those Things That You Can Afford

When you have a credit card in hand, it can get really tempting, and you start buying whatever you think you want. If not, then don't buy it now. Make a goal to save the money required for purchasing that item instead of buying it on credit.

Don't Transfer Balance If Not Necessary

Some people have this habit of clearing their balance with a higher credit card but such repeated balance transferring can actually backfire at you. When you keep transferring balanced without keeping track of your activities, you might end up with an ever- increasing balance and you will also have to clear the fee requires for all those transfers.

Try Not Taking out a Cash Advance

Sometimes, you may be in the moment, and you were not thinking clearly so, you decide to take a cash advance. Moreover, you will have to realize that you are getting into credit card debt if you have started making cash advanced. The moment you see it happening, you will have to start working on that emergency fund and also tweak your budget.

Lastly, I would like to say that no matter how many measures you take, try avoiding increasing your credit cards unnecessarily because the more the number of credit cards, the more you will have to stop yourself from overspending.

Conclusion

If you want to repair your credit then here are some steps that might be more effective. The first step is to gather your finances together and make a budget. Sometimes the problem isn't about paying what you owe so much as it is about priorities. Next, save up an emergency fund of at least $1000 in case of any unexpected expenses that pop up in the future. Next, tackle the collection agencies. Many of them will work with you if you explain your situation, and are willing to pay less than the full amount if you can afford it. It might be worth looking into a credit counselor as sometimes they can help with creditors and make things easier on your financial situation.

Credit repair service is a process that creates an accurate financial history for a customer and helps to increase their credit score. One of the ways in which your credit score can be increased is by obtaining new loans, paying off old loans, and making payments on time. A good credit score will give you access to better interest rates as well as other financial services.

Your credit score will be scarred regardless if they fix it or not. And, because the credit repair company is charging you a fee to fix your score, the chances are that you will have to pay for their services in the future. There are many websites out there that will list top credit repair companies, and while some of them work, some of them are just trying to get your money. In addition, some people think the credit repair companies are legitimate and then end up paying for their services anyways. It is the easiest solution because you can pick up phone calls from these companies, but be careful. You have to make sure that you do not give any personal contact information to these credit repair companies because they are fakes. If you want to use a credit repair company, do some research on your own before you give them any personal Information? If you are not sure about the credit repair company, then you can go to the Better Business Bureau and see how many complaints they have. Also, check the state department's website for complaints against the company. If there are hundreds of complaints that they are a scamming company then do not give them any money. Trust me, it is better to be safe than sorry.

You may be in denial about the state of your credit, but if you are planning on applying for any loans or credit cards, it is imperative that you try and fix. Nowadays people rely on their credit scores more than ever before to determine their eligibility for loans and other types of credit. Such companies are highly skilled in the art of repairing credit, and can help you avoid some of the most common pitfalls. If you have suffered a serious hit to your score due to late payments or bankruptcies, it could take years before your score is restored to its former glory. That's because it takes time for your creditors to update their records with your current status, you should pay off any outstanding debts and make your payments on time. If you have made a few late payments recently, or have otherwise damaged your credit score, contact the creditor or consumer reporting agency. Explain that you have had some trouble recently, but you are now working to rectify the situation and would like to make a payment arrangement. Many creditors and agencies will work with consumers who show a sincere desire to repay their debts.

Finally, my opinion on the best way to improve your credit is to make a budget for yourself and stick to it! If you can avoid doing that, then your credit will be in great shape.

Lightning Source UK Ltd.
Milton Keynes UK
UKHW020750080822
406990UK00001B/5